Compass of the Technical School

Table of Contents

Foreword

Chapter 1:

Why Getting Into Technical School Is The Right Decision?

Chapter 2:

Deciding Your Career Path First

Chapter 3:

Search For Technical School With Accreditation

Chapter 4:

Understanding Admission Requirement In Important

Chapter 5:

You Can Pay A Visit To The Campus

Chapter 6:

Make Sure There Is Sufficient Class Available

Chapter 7:

Seeking And Research On Technical School From Internet

Chapter 8:

Is Online Technical School For You?

Chapter 9:

Checking Out The Course Fee To Ensure You Can Afford

Chapter 10:

Choosing Technical School With Occupational Guidance

Terms and Conditions

LEGAL NOTICE

The Publisher has strived to be as accurate and complete as possible in the creation of this report, notwithstanding the fact that he does not warrant or represent at any time that the contents within are accurate due to the rapidly changing nature of the Internet.

While all attempts have been made to verify information provided in this publication, the Publisher assumes no responsibility for errors, omissions, or contrary interpretation of the subject matter herein. Any perceived slights of specific persons, peoples, or organizations are unintentional.

In practical advice books, like anything else in life, there are no guarantees of income made. Readers are cautioned to reply on their own judgment about their individual circumstances to act accordingly.

This book is not intended for use as a source of legal, business, accounting
or financial advice. All readers are advised to seek services of competent
professionals in legal, business, accounting and finance fields.

You are encouraged to print this book for easy reading.

Foreword

With the current state of economy, more and more high school students are shunning from the thought of pursuing a four-year degree in a university or college. However, it does not necessarily mean that you need to stop chasing your dreams and be contented with being a high school graduate. Right now, you have the choice to enroll in trade schools or also known as technical schools where you can learn some things and earn a certification to help you in reaching your goals and be successful in your life.

In this book, you can learn all that you need to know in order to find the best technical schools in town that will help you in securing a brighter future ahead of you.

Technical School Compass

Your Guide To Find The Best Technical Schools In Town

Chapter 1

Why Getting Into Technical School Is The Right Decision?

Synopsis

Why is it a good thing for you to enter a technical school at this point in time? What can you get out of it? How will it change your life and help you shape your future? In this chapter, learn the benefits that you can enjoy when you get into a technical school.

If you are already close to the completion of your high school years, it is possible that at this point, you are already contemplating on which university or college you will attend. Without a doubt, there are various benefits that you can get when you graduate from universities or colleges, the first of which is a high pay. But you might not be familiar with the fact that right now, there are also different kinds of schools that you can enter after you graduated from high school, ranging from 2-year community colleges, to the usual 4-year universities and the technical schools with certificate programs.

The Perks of Completing a Technical School Program

The last might not be familiar to you but just so you know, there are also plenty of benefits that you can enjoy when you enroll in one of the programs they offer. Here are these benefits that will surely make you confident that the decision you make in joining them is the right one.

Specific Career Plans

Among the best benefits of technical schools that you might not consider at first is that such schools provide specific career plans. For sure, you have heard about some of your relatives and friends who are graduates from universities and colleges but were never successful finding a good job in the field of their choice. Sadly, this scenario happens when the degree you choose is fairly general. There are several students who find it hard to transfer and their educational experience to the experienced in the real world, all because of the broad studies they had.

Good thing that when you attend a technical school, you get the chance of training in a certain area that can lead you to a specific career plan. Majority of technical schools offer certificates in some of the career fields that are highly in demand, including IT, business and healthcare. This training that is job specific helps you land a job right away after your graduation.

Less Expense

For sure, you are very much aware how expensive higher education is but chances are you do not have an idea of how much every kind of university or college is going to cost you during the length of the program or degree that you choose. From educational expenses, to living expenses as well as other miscellaneous expenses, all of these will be a burden that you need to carry on your shoulders for the entire four years of your education, adding up every single year. But by choosing to enter a technical school, the expenses that you are going to encounter will be lesser because the programs they offer require shorter completion times, which helps you save great amounts of money along the way.

Hands-On Learning

The last but definitely not the least benefit of technical schools is your chance of getting hands-on learning. It is said that there are various ways to learn, including tactile, auditory and visual to meet today's demands in the quickly growing industries. If you are a person who learns better when you do something physical, you will be a good fit for a technical school. All students tend to enjoy not just by hearing how things are done but by actually performing their skills and participating using their own hands.

These are only a few of the benefits that you can get once you join a technical school but with this short list, you can say that entering one is definitely one of the best decisions that you will ever make in your life.

Chapter 2

Deciding Your Career Path First

Synopsis

Entering a technical school is not a spur of the moment decision. Before you apply, you need to be sure first if this is really the path that you want to take, if it is really the one thing that will lead you to the kind of life that you want. In this chapter, you will learn tips on how to best determine the career path that you need to take.

As you fill up the college application forms, you will surely wonder if you are really making the right choice, if this is really the career path that you want to take. Choosing the correct career path is truly confusing and hard, more because with the current state of economy, competition has soared higher. Should you join a regular university or will a technical school be a more practical choice?

For this task to be much easier, there are some tips that can help you in your decision making.

Choose the Best Career Path That Suits You – Tips to Help You Out

Stick to What Interests You

When you choose the right career path that suits you, the very first and most vital thing that should be remembered is your interests. Forget about the high paying and in demand jobs first as it might make you choose the wrong path. If your interest lies on the bottom of the list of high paying jobs, follow what your heart dictates you. Cheesy as it may sound, it has been proven time and time again that doing something you love increases your chances of excelling in your chosen field, and before you know it, money is going to follow right after.

Know Your Qualities and Skills

It is one aspect that is usually taken for granted by most people. Some might even assume that they lack the skills, something that is completely untrue. There are those who have inborn leadership skills, while others are meant to become followers. No matter which category you belong to, you are still meant to excel in the field that you chose.

As for the qualities, focus on how you respond to specific situations. Do you aim for perfection? Is pressure something you find easy to deal with? The answers you make to the questions can help you in figuring out the next step once you have identified your interests.

Don't Rush

Never choose a career path only because your friends are going for it or your parents are pressuring you. As much as possible, take time out so that you can figure out what you would really want to do. Clear your mind and do whatever it is that you need to do to identify the kind of career that will give you fulfillment and true happiness.

Remember these tips to know if the programs offered in technical school are really the right career path for you to take.

Chapter 3

Search For Technical School With Accreditation

Synopsis

Why is it that you need to look for technical schools that have an accreditation? What does an accreditation signify? Does it have anything to do with the kind of education that you can expect to get from a school? Learn why you need to search for accredited technical schools in this chapter.

If you have finally decided that the career path that you want to take will be easier when you enter a technical school, the next thing that you need to do is to search for schools that have been accredited.

Accreditation can actually offer various essential benefits, including the following:

Why Accreditation Matters

- This can put an approval stamp on the graduates. When you have graduated from accredited institutions, it will indicate that you are prepared to practice at certain levels.

  - This will provide educational programs that have opportunities for self-reflection and self-definition, together with feedback on the program direction and content.

  - This paves the way for the chance of continuous improvement of both educational programs and institutions.

Accreditation serves as the protection of the interests not just of students but also their parents, the academic institution itself, as well as the potential employers through assuring that all educational programs being offered were able to successfully attain a level that can meet or even exceed the standards that have been developed by the field's experts.

Even though joining an accredited technical school will ensure that you will be a successful professional after you have graduated, still, it can guarantee that as a student, you were able to demonstrate a particular set of abilities and skills as reflected on the criteria of accreditation. While this is not an adequate condition for a professional success, in majority of disciplines, this acts as a necessary condition.

That is why when you look for a technical school, always check if it is accredited or not in order for you to enjoy the benefits that it offers.

Chapter 4

Understanding Admission Requirement In Important

Synopsis

After searching for an accredited technical school, the next important step is for you to prepare your admission requirements. It is important that all of these will be prepared ahead of time and more importantly, you also need to understand them so that you will know what their unique purposes and uses are. This chapter will teach you more about these admission requirements and why they are needed in the first place.

Throughout your high school years, the process of admission becomes even more intense than ever. Seniors are busy in writing their applications, retaking the standardized tests, finalizing their list of colleges and generally getting anxious as to whether or not they will get it. On the other hand, the juniors are on to their PSAT, the first visits in colleges and what is considered to be their academic lives' hardest year.

Reduce Your Stress on Your Admission Requirements

Practically everyone is keen on meeting the admission requirements. But if you chose to enter a technical school instead of a traditional college or university, how will you maintain your sanity, find your right path, and put the whole process into the correct perspective?

First and foremost, you have to remember that you are the one in control. The process of admission itself is about searching for schools that will fit you well then doing the best you can to get in. While others, namely your parents, siblings, friends, and teachers, tell you that you better get this or that, you must always be in the driver's seat who will make decisions about the colleges, standardized tests and classes.

When it comes to understanding the admission requirement, the most crucial thing you need to bear in mind is that this must showcase who you really are. Just be yourself. Never do things for the sake of college alone. Do not put on a mask so you can impress a school. Keep things real and communicate in such a way that your true personality will shine out.

The last but not the least important thing is to completely understand the admission requirements themselves. This will save you the trouble of having to go back again and again just to complete everything. If possible, check out the website of the school if it has one and get a list of all their requirements. Complete them the soonest that you can so that you will no longer have to worry when you finally go to the campus and submit your admission requirements.

Chapter 5

You Can Pay A Visit To The Campus

Synopsis

While you're too intent on finding a good technical school, why don't you allot some of your time in visiting the campus of your prospect school? Do you know that doing so can give you numerous benefits? Yes, there are benefits to paying a visit to a school campus and this chapter discusses some of them.

While the websites of different technical schools and the brochures they give out can be pretty helpful and informative, the perfect way for you to get to learn more about a school is by paying a visit to the campus itself.

The Benefits of Paying a Visit to a Technical School Campus

For you to get the ideal sense of what the life in the campus is like at a certain technical school, you might want to set a schedule for your visit when the classes are in session. It will give you the chance of observing both the students and the faculty inside the classroom and how they interact within the campus.

In case the school is far from your home yet you still feel determined to apply there, it will also be a smart idea if you will set an interview with the admission officer on the same day of your visit.

Even though the officials of the school can provide you with a single perspective on the learning experience in their school, it might also be best if you can actually know the thoughts of the present students there.

The perfect way of doing this is by scheduling an overnight stay in the campus dormitory. Through this, you can get the opportunity of eating with the students in their dining hall or attending the activities in the campus and asking the students about their life in the campus. Try to find out about the things that they like and love the most about the technical school as well as the specific aspects that they do not find enthusiastic about the place. Also, you can use all of the impressions and information that you have acquired during your campus visit to serve as your guide when you will finally decide if you would like to go on with the next step, which is to apply.

Chapter 6

Make Sure There Is Sufficient Class Available

Synopsis

Technical schools have now become highly in demand as more and more high school graduates choose to pursue skill specific programs that will help them in entering their chosen field in an easier way. During your search for a technical school, it is important to ensure that the classes are sufficient so that you will not have any issues in joining one.

Economic recession and the slow recovery period that followed took its toll on graduate schools and colleges yet there remains to be one illuminating spot in the sector of education: technical schools.

Vocational and career technical education schools have experienced a remarkable increase in their enrollments just when graduate schools noticed a decline in their student applications.

Set Your Technical School Class Ahead of Time

It has been projected by the Bureau of Labor Statistics that the middle skill jobs or those that generally call for some sufficient training and education more than high school but less than bachelor's degrees are going to make up around 45% of all the job openings in this year 2014. Out of the jobs that require postsecondary education, the ones that require an associate degree have been expected to have the fastest growth at around 19%.

According to experts, a lot of vocational programs witnessed such a sharp boost in the number of their enrollments that there are many students who might end up getting wait listed because of overcrowding.

Right at this moment, there are just plenty of careers that call for a 2-year degree or a certificate and most of these careers actually pay wages that are above average in areas including construction, architecture and manufacturing. Such opportunities can give you the chance of earning a substantial middle income wage yet at the same time, you are also expected to have the right skills set.

The increase in the interest on technical schools actually spans all experience levels and ages – from the high school students, to the graduates of 4 year college, as well as adults who have decided to return to school for the purpose of upgrading their skills so that they can stay employable.

Even though technical programs are more hands on compared to the courses in a traditional college, you must never dismiss them as something easy. As said earlier, these programs call for specific set of skills and for you to successfully complete them, you need to be ready for facing any kind of challenges along the way.

While some critics of technical schools claim that the high school graduates limit the career options they have when they enroll on a program that is focused on a single trade, experts say that students always have the chance of going back to the traditional career so that they can continue their existing education.

Due to the doors of opportunities that will be opened to the students once they decide to enter technical schools, the classes have become crowded. For this reason, it is important that before you decide on a technical school, you first need to check if there is still sufficient class available where you can join. In order to know this, you can either pay a visit to the campus itself or you can also check the official website of the school.

As technical schools become more in demand, getting into them can now become a bit tougher. So, make sure that you do your research so that you will know everything there is to know before you apply.

Chapter 7

Seeking And Research On Technical School From Internet

Synopsis

The internet has definitely become the perfect place where you can look for in order to learn all the information you want to learn about one thing, and technical schools are not exempted. Right now, looking for these schools and getting to know more about them is made easier than ever with the use of the internet.

Today's generation has been extensively exposed to the different uses of technology and students of today have found out that the internet is their new best friend for so many reasons.

If you are still undecided as to what technical school you can enter in, the best way to find the one that best suits you is by conducting an online research.

Search Online for Your Prospect Technical Schools

Right now, a single search for the phrase "technical school" can give you thousands of results in a matter of seconds. In order to make your search for area specific, particularly when you want to know those schools that are close to your home town, all you need to do is to include the name of the place in your search.

Then, once you have a list of the schools nearby or in the specific place where you plan to study, the next thing to do is to check out their website. In the official website of technical schools, you can find all the information that you might want to know, starting from the history of the school, to the programs they offer, their facilities and amenities, the number of students, and many other important facts and details that might be of interest to any potential student.

You have to take note of all these pieces of information as these will be able to help you in determining if a certain school fits your needs and requirements or if it does not.

You also need to know their contact information so that you can easily place a call or send an email if ever you have some inquiries. You also need to check if they are accredited by the corresponding bodies. It might also be a good idea for you to see if their website contains the list of requirements for admission so that you can prepare the needed documents beforehand.

Conducting an online search on technical schools is definitely the easiest and most convenient way in order for you to determine the school that suits you best.

Chapter 8

Is Online Technical School For You?

===

Synopsis

Once you are done with your online search for technical schools, you have probably discovered that there are actually online technical schools. Is it something suitable for you? Will it be able to help you in reaching your goals? Learn more about online technical schools in this chapter.

Discover More About Online Technical Schools

Online technical schools offer certificate and degree programs that give students the chance of entering the workforce in a timely and cheaper manner compared to other schools and programs. The programs focus on training and education on specific careers with no excessive requirements for general studies and electives. Here, the graduates are being prepared for an immediate placement at entry level in their chosen field.

Overview of Online Technical Schools

A technical school or also known as vocational school or trade school is a kind of school where the enrollees are thought of how to perform certain tasks with practical applications. University and college curricula can include broad topics on interdisciplinary course. But, the online technical school programs are usually focusing on all the activities on the job specific and marketable skills. Online technical schools are basically technical schools that exclusively offer their curriculum through methods of distance learning with the use of the internet.

What Types of Programs are Offered by Online Technical Schools?

Technical schools may either offer various unrelated programs or they can also focus on a specific training field like cosmetology, culinary arts, allied health practices, auto repair or technology. Study areas in a umbrella schools can include education, criminal justice, interior design, graphic design, photography, nursing, computer technology or computer animation.

Today, online technical schools have become even more popular because of schedule flexibility and accessibility. Even though the programs are hosted primarily online, there are several courses that call for experiential elements. There are differences when it comes to the requirements for satisfying these hands on elements by program and school. There are students that can pursue a local internship or their can also work with approved mentors. The students in such schools are prepared for entering the workforce right away after their graduation.

Comparing Technical School Degrees and University and College Degrees

There are a few differences between the degree programs offered by technical schools and those offered by universities and colleges. Variables can include subject matter, length and pricing. Achieving a technical school degree can only take 30 weeks as much as 2 years, which happens to be lesser time compared to other degrees. Since the programs in online technical schools are more flexible when it comes to price and schedule, the students can attain a degree faster or even slower as compared to going through the whole program based in a campus. The public technical schools usually carry lower tuition costs compared to the private ones.

The quality of degrees in technical schools can never be considered lower than other kinds of degrees' quality. The only big different between the schools that offer the typical 2 or 4 year degrees and trade schools is the specificity of the subject matter that the students can learn. Graduates of technical schools are regarded to be highly trained and more specialized.

Chapter 9

Checking Out The Course Fee To Ensure You Can Afford

Synopsis

Education, whether you like it or not, comes with a cost, literally speaking. Just like when applying for the traditional colleges or universities, it is also important for you to check first if you can really afford the course fee at technical schools or you need to start looking for an alternative that will be easy on your pocket.

Paying for Technical Schools – What You Need to Know

While paying for 4 year college and shorter certificate or degree program has some similarities, there are also several crucial differences that you need to remember.

Technical schools are focused on career-specific training in certain fields like electronics, criminal justice, accounting, and nursing. By conducting a little research and completely understanding how technical schools operate, you will surely improve your chances of looking for quality education even at a fair and affordable price.

The Price of Technical School Education

A technical school or also referred to as trade school or vocational school focuses on skill learning instead of studying a certain major. There are instances when the fees and tuition at trade schools can be higher compared to the price of that of a program in two year college. But in most cases, technical schools can be a much better deal. To know the possible expenses that you will incur along the way, it is a important that you also do your homework so that you can identify the specific type of program that will fit your budget.

Before Signing the Dotted Line

Once you have chosen a specific technical school, make you that you read carefully the enrolment contract and understand all the costs stated within. You have to remember, however, that you never find such a thing as a guaranteed job much less a guaranteed salary once you have graduated.

Any claims to the opposite will surely be a good reason for you to be skeptical.

You need to take some time on investigating the specific programs that are of interest to you. First of all, check whether or not the school of your choice is accredited by the concerned agency or government body. As mentioned in Chapter 3, accreditation will not only signify a school's legitimacy for it also means that the students who have attended and will attend the specific school are eligible for financial aid.

Second, you also have to ask regarding the number of students who were able to find employment in the trade that they have chosen and ask for contact information of the other graduates so that you will learn if the education they got helped them or not.

Should you discover that the course of your choice is not within your budget, it does not necessarily mean that you can no longer enroll for there are not financial aids available for students. By learning about these aids as well as student loans and grants, you will surely find it easier to pursue your technical school education.

Chapter 10

Choosing Technical School With Occupational Guidance

Occupational guidance is the last but definitely not the least consideration when searching for technical schools. Why is it important for your education? How will it be able to help you? Learn the answers to these and more in this last chapter of your quest for the right technical school for you.

For the modern generation, the present holds a special significance. It has become an era of thousands of changes, when new ideals have been proposed and even more new patterns have emerged. This era of utter independence combined with the incessant changes have dramatically changed the way on how schools pursue their aims. These changes that symbolize progress calls for an urgent reorientation of the students' attitudes as far as jobs are concerned. In the complex process of having to mop up the age old cobwebs of sheer prejudice against the blue collar professions and occupational information's dissemination, schools definitely need to a play a very crucial role.

Back in the earlier days in the entire complicated and complex field of education, it can be noticed that if there is one aspect that has been greatly neglected, it is none other than occupational guidance. But thank to the education authorities' foresight and dynamism, the students now have sufficient opportunities of gaining adequate occupational information for them to be properly equipped when looking for a job that will suit their aptitude and overall ability. A graduate student who does not have even the smallest idea regarding the job that is going to take up after leaving school will likely fall into a taste of flux, with the imminent danger that he will go for the wrong job and end up in complete despair. Right now, with the help of occupational guidance, students who will soon be leaving school with at least have a vague idea of those jobs that they plan to take up.

Every single year, there is an increasing number of students who quit schooling. Thus, it is a must that the young citizens will be properly guided in choosing the right career once they graduate. A newly graduate who simply plunges blindly to a certain job that does not suit him or one that he is not interested in will find himself a round peg within a square hole. This is something that no country will be able to afford that is why it is of paramount importance for all students to be properly guided when choosing a career for them to contribute their maximum to the whole society.

Even today when almost everything is done through automation, around 2/3 of the life of men is still spent working, with the career choice something very delicate for them to tackle. If you made the wrong choice, you will be spending your whole life in a world of incessant frustration. Usually, the very first job that a new graduate lands on becomes his only one during his entire working career. It means that unless you are suited and contented with your current job, you are never going to be happy.

Thus, occupational guidance is very important for its primary aim is to assist students in making a choice on their career based on their interests, training, and aptitudes.

So, during your search for technical schools, make sure that you go for one that offers occupational guidance.

www.ingramcontent.com/pod-product-compliance
Lightning Source LLC
LaVergne TN
LVHW020454080526
838202LV00055B/5447